In Honor of Isaac Tinu George,
Binu George, Aleysa George, Rosamma George
and all those we have lost too soon.

Caden, Xavier, Silas and Tinu - you are always loved, wanted, and needed. You are a daily reminder of God's goodness and grace. Isaac is always with you.
.

# Isaac's Red Balloon

By Asha George

Illustrated By Aparna Pandey

As the morning breeze flows
through my window,
I hear the songs
as the blue jays play.

I smile!

Today is my sweet angel brother Isaac's heavenly birthday!

I am sad Isaac is not with us,
but I'll keep his memory alive...

by sharing hugs

and sending red balloons

into the evening sky.

I wonder all about him,
now that he is seven.
I dream of the fun things we will do
when we meet in Heaven!

Will we play soccer,
tag,
or a game of tug-of-war?

Maybe we will go hiking,
be superheroes,
and do so much more!

I feel close to Isaac when I draw pictures, and share my feelings with my mother.

We will tell stories
and release red balloons
to honor my sweet angel brother.

The sun has set
and the moon shines
with a beautiful glow.

Mama grabs the red balloons and says, "Outside we shall go!"

We step outside together,
closely we will stand,
each with a precious red balloon
held tightly in hand.

We say a prayer, we yell a cheer, shouting aloud,

"We love you, Isaac dear!"

We chase the red balloons
as they soar up high,
flying away
into the starlit sky.

I imagine floating up,
rising with my red balloon,

and meeting my angel brother
above the bright crescent moon.

As his birthday celebrations come to an end,

we look at pictures sent to us from family and friends!

I feel Isaac close to me
through their kindness and love.

I know he is with us,
watching from Heaven up above.

Do you miss a special person, like I miss my sweet brother?

Just remember,
they are safe and close
in your heart forever.

In our dreams

we will see our angels soon,

smiling and laughing...

...holding our red balloons!

**Grief** is a reaction you have when you lose someone, something, or some place important to you. As you experience grief, you may feel sad, angry, relief, afraid, shocked, guilty, disappointed, overwhelmed, confused, anxious, love, regretful, and/or hopeful.

Continue the dialogue with children. The complexity of grief and missing someone changes over time.. Therefore, it's important to talk to children to affirm their changing emotions and discuss confusing thoughts, questions, or feelings that could cause distress.

# Acknowledgements

To my parents and siblings, thank you for your support and prayers. I hope this book can help you feel close to your special angels too.

To Naya, Ava, Naveen, Jude, Anna, and Luke: You guys are amazing cousins! You bring so much joy to us! Always remember, Isaac is with you.

To my friends and family, thank you for remembering Isaac, for saying his name, and celebrating his life. Thank you for all the laughter and love. We couldn't do this journey without you.

To Elizabeth K'mali, for inspiring me to believe in myself and write this book!

To Andrea Dunning, thank you for sharing the idea of releasing balloons for Isaac.

To Lindsay Black., Patricia Chambers, Ashley Kuruvilla, and Hannah Gyani, thank you for proofreading and editing multiple times! Thank you for your suggestions, encouragement, and keeping me sane.

To Aparna Pandey, for beautifully illustrating exactly what my heart envisioned. Thank you for listening to me even though we are oceans apart.

To Caden, thank you for being the best big brother. Thank you for all your help in writing this book. Thank you for sharing your heart with me. I promise to always protect it. Isaac is always protecting his big brother.

To Xavier, thank you for your creativity and passion. Thank you for showing me how to care for people and love deeply. Thank you for all your artistic advice in this book. I promise to always encourage you and be your number one fan. Isaac lives in your heart. Not only are you his brother, but you are also his best friend!

To Silas, thank you for your joy. Your smile lights up the room. Thank you for loving Isaac. I wish I was there to watch you both play together in heaven. God created you perfectly to restore our joy. I promise to always celebrate in your joy. Isaac loves to see his baby brother laugh.

To Tinu, thank you for formatting this book multiple times. Thank you for serving and loving me. Even when it feels like our world is falling apart, you stand firm on God's truth, and I can lean on you. Thank you for being my rock.

## A Word From The Author

Dear Readers,

When Isaac passed away in 2014, the emotions of grief were overwhelming. I longed to feel a connection with Isaac. I knew I needed to do something to keep my son's memory alive, and to feel close to him. Often, after someone passes away, people stop saying their names. I needed Isaac's name to be spoken. Even though he died, he was very much alive in our hearts. My other children, Caden, Xavier and Silas were grieving too. I wanted to create a tangible connection that my boys, husband, and I needed to help with our journey through grief.. In October of 2014, I posted a quote for Pregnancy and Infant Loss Month. A dear friend, saw my post and suggested picking a day in October and releasing balloons in honor of Isaac! It was tangible, as if we were sending our balloons to our angel; it helped us feel a connection with him; and it was a joyful celebration. From that day forward, October 17th became Isaac's day. The grief we have will forever be there, but it is changing. Our vision slowly changed from focusing on our pain to focusing on the goodness we have even in our pain. Now we are using our pain to help others. Isaac's Red Balloon is a true story of how we found hope in our grief. It's amazing to see how God continues to make beauty out of our ashes. I hope our story can help restore a sense of hope, and help you feel close to your special loved ones.

Asha George

Please visit www.atgeorge.com to learn more about Isaac's Red Balloon

©2021 Asha George.
All rights reserved. Except for brief excerpts for review purposes, no part of this book may be reproduced or used in any form except by written permission from the author.

Made in the USA
Monee, IL
24 March 2022